What Water Does at a Time Like This

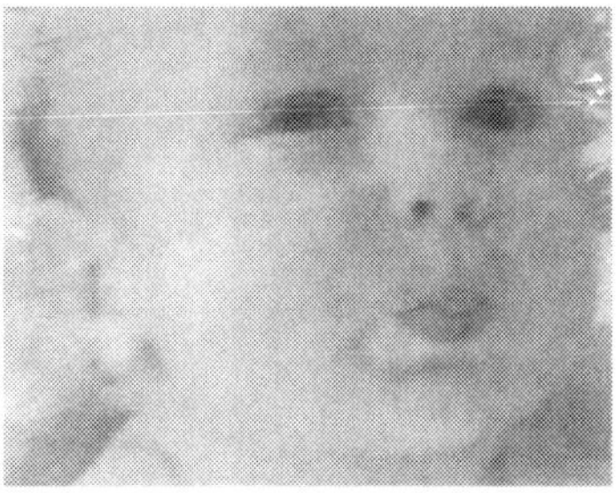

Contents

The Slope

The Jealous Gods	5
Take It to the Lord in Prayer	6
These Believers	7
Judgment Day	8
The Business of Crows	9
On the Job	11
Go Back, Go Back	12
Man on Ice	13
Why Did the Hawk Cross the Road?	15

The Seven Pools

The First Day	19
Waterbabies	20
The Old Masters	21
The Philosophy of the Motel Pool	22
One Night on Bainbridge Island	23
The Back Float	24
It Can Be Anything	25

Ghost Trees

What Can You Say Now? How Can You Say It?	29
Farewell to John Fahey's Guitar	30
In the Afterlife	31
The Tourists	32
Missing Richard	33
Little Finger	34
My Mother Is in the Trunk	35
Meeting the Night Visitors	36
Waking from the Dream of Obligation & Progress	37
She Falls for It Over & Over	38
In the Last Place	40
Heart's Desire	41
What You Can Say to Me When I'm Dead	42

The Winter Solstice	43
After the Fire	44
Dolmen	46
Drâa Valley Cemetery	47

White Scar

Vapor Trail	51
Come Again?	52
As I Walked Out One Morning	53
Foreign	54
The Kon Tum Motorbike Taxi Driver	55
Everything But the Squeal	56
Sukulen, the Predictor	57
The Legless Shoeshine Man	59
Cut-Away View of a Trailer South of Mérida	60
Now You See It, Now You Don't	62
The Town at the Bottom of the Reservoir	63
What a World	64
Dans le Jardin El Harti, Marrakech	65

The Terrible Confusion of Light

Good News	69
The Nature Poem	70
Nice Hat	71
Out of Season	73
Greeting the Hummingbirds	74
Origami	75
Loggerheads	76
The Boys	77
The Hiroshima Day Sidewalk Silhouettes	78
These Others	79
Resolution	81
Acknowledgments & Notes	83
About the Author	87

For Marquita, always.

What Water Does at a Time Like This

The Slope

The Jealous Gods

When He made the Big Bang
the rest of us told Him how splendid it was,
but we really meant it should have been bigger,

could have tossed its particles farther,
ought to have made a much louder sound.
We meant it didn't look like much so far,

just a lot of little sparkles in the infinite dark.
So He said it wasn't even finished yet.
He said it was still expanding and anyway

He was the one who had gone to all the trouble
of putting it together, so we might as well
shove off. Which is pretty much what we did.

Naturally, we had to use the rest of our floods first,
and thunderbolts and swarming clouds of locusts,
but every single time we did, it was a disaster.

Nothing truly epochal ever happened.
Then eventually the calendar caught up with us,
and after that our days were numbered.

Take It to the Lord in Prayer

When it looks like He might have been
stacking baskets of darkness along one side
of the sky's warehouse and reaching
His long finger through a slot in the far wall
to switch on the poplar trees and make them shine,
to light up the seagull so it blazes white
against that deep and negative ceiling,

you have to stop whatever you were doing.
You have to wonder what would happen
if He stuck to His needles this time and finally
darned the black holes logic keeps poking through
His starry socks. Either that or unraveled
the ball of old yarns from which He is
supposed to have stitched up all the mysteries.
By God, you say, then we'd really have some answers.

These Believers

People who believe in God have got it
easy: they have one answer for everything.
Why human beings came
to have a tailbone and yet no tail.
Or why, despite repeated lessons to the contrary,
whole nations persist in thinking they can win at war.

Or how morning's first light can turn
even the slash piles and stumps on a clearcut slope
to gold or rose, redeeming them for a moment.
The eye, these believers say, is God's thimble,
and light is what God stitches with.

The rest of us are more practical.
Necessity dictates, we explain:
humans have more use for thumbs than tails.
Revenge is sweet; the world turns on it.
And light, we say, light is nothing
but the other half of shadow.

Judgment Day

What he saw when he saw his own face
in the artificial glare of the restroom
mirror was not the man he had in mind.

Pardon me, he said to himself,
and when the automatic water spilled
out of its fixture, he washed his hands

of the other man—his knowing expression,
his familiar gesture—checking his fly
before he stepped into the public sunlight.

The Business of Crows

One of them has a discarded
half-pint milk carton
by its pinched top

and is banging it on the sidewalk.
Hopping with it, dragging it along,
he hefts it with his beak

and swings it against the concrete.
Then he pauses to inspect his work,
to adjust his grip before

picking up the carton
and smacking it down again.
Every time he hits the sidewalk

with the empty box
it makes a flat, satisfying *plop*.
Perhaps that's all the crow wants,

the hollow report
he gets for his labor
confirming its emptiness.

As for me, I have stopped
on the way back to my office
to watch a crow's involvement

with a milk carton. Sunlight,
filtering through bare trees,
stains the bird a dark blue

that slips to black
like secret ink and makes sense
only as his feathers move.

What could possibly be
more important than this?
I have no further excuses.

On the Job

At work, Sisyphus
rolls up his sleeves, they roll back
down. He hitches up

his jeans, they ride down again.
He tugs his jeans up, they slip

right back down. He says
fuck it and begins pushing
his stone up the slope.

Go Back, Go Back

Whine of my neighbor's
power saw cutting, binding
a little, bogging

down, then biting in
again. I can almost smell
the sawdust, pungent

pine resin or dry
walnut lingering, filling
the shop. My uncle's

voice rising with it
from his absence, saying *Well . . .*
because he always

started a sentence
like an afterthought, *maybe
you better measure*

again. So I have
to stop. Here comes the nagging
blade of doubt, the same

circular reason
I've never been able to
finish anything.

Man on Ice

The road swings left
but the obstinate car keeps aiming straight
toward frosted hemlocks and Douglas firs
that crowd the shoulder like
spectators at a cold parade.

It is not their nature
to jump out of the way,
and knowing this the driver of the car
would be praying if he could.
Maybe something is happening in heaven anyway,

something the driver is not allowed to see:
the turning of circumstances,
the absolution of certain problematic acts,
the shifting of minimums so that even this
insignificant driver might be saved.

The driver, however, is wringing the steering wheel,
screaming, as the commonplace simile has it,
like a motherfucker, thus
disguising any metaphysical
interference in such a way

that he might later say he had helped himself,
while in the meantime, a sermon
from the pulpit in his brain
declaims on his life
as a chain of accidents,

of one thing sliding into another,
like his car on ice
weighing in against the trees,

or the way he first met his wife, slipping
into the seat next to hers in a crowded theater,

or what got him into this predicament,
his turning off the freeway to stay out of traffic,
then drifting over the gentle swell of the road
as if his car were a boat being swept out to sea;
and in one sudden reduction of logic

he sees the whole of existence
as simultaneous action and
its equal opposite—bang & recoil,
tort & retort, a ball
flattening against God's racquet strings,

then springing away from the point of impact,
from the grip, the swing, the wrist snap,
the follow-through—
and he wants to write this down before it poofs
into nothing but

right now he is too busy blaspheming
irresistibly toward immovable trees,
strangling the helm
of his rudderless vessel.
Right now he's really got his hands full.

Why Did the Hawk Cross the Road?

A moment's notice means no time
to think, means this is it, right now, and in this
moment—feathers up close and no place to swerve,
another car coming on in the facing lane, sunlight
flaring across its windshield, and otherwise ditch,
barbwire fence, power lines poling the roadside—

thinking isn't what you do, but you do
see the little shift in the wing, the tail, the way
primaries finger air while your own fingers
clench, grip, your jaw tight, right foot automatically
pumping once, quick, and just as quick
letting go. Nobody hitting anything.

How does that happen, that stretching
of the instant so you hold it though it's too fast
to catch? What happens to the other narrative track
with its collision, blood and broken glass,
its strobing emergency lights, sirens
ripping the fabric of the afternoon?

Somewhere else paramedics must be squeezing
their hands into latex gloves. Somewhere else
elastic moments may snap like that and stop,
but here you are, witness to a miracle: a bird
turning into pure reflex. A flinch. Later you'll say
Out of nowhere. Later you'll say *And gone*.

The Seven Pools

The First Day

Saturday morning the pool fills
with children. Their parents
want them to learn something
preposterous: not just to tread water,
but to move through it as easily as they run
at home from one room to another. Naturally
the miracle of flotation escapes some of them;

however, the believers, buoyant in their faith,
hold their breath and push away from the side.
Face down, arms outstretched, these blessed ones
glide like angels in a fleeting state of grace,
then pop up grinning when they run out of air.
Splashed with success, they hug themselves
happily in the blue-lipped chill.

Meanwhile, the few still clinging to the wall
watch their own number shrink. Small, miserable,
suspicious of their parents for making them
suffer here, they begin to see the arrangement
of things: how easily everyone can turn
away from them when they don't give in,
how lonely a personal conviction is.

Waterbabies

What do the babies think
as they go under? Their mothers,
who would surely walk across the surface of the pool
to save them, now smile and coo
and dunk them. When the babies come up
sputtering, their mothers give them wet kisses,
hug them soothingly, and dunk them again.

Some of the babies laugh and splash,
and some stare up in quiet astonishment,
but most of them struggle,
pumping their legs the way frogs do,
trying to jump. The cries that fly
from their wide mouths bounce off the ceiling
and fall in a shattered chorus back to the water.

The mothers just want their babies to grow up
safely. They wrap them in towels,
cuddle them. But the babies
are learning to hold their breath
as if they might have seen the way
their mothers smiled as they pulled them down
beneath the surface of their first betrayal.

The Old Masters

In the YMCA locker room
they move deliberately, the two of them,
neatly hanging their pants in their lockers,
stepping into their swimming trunks
the same way they walk across the tiled
shower floor: not quite like men on ice
but balancing, ready like that.

The taller one has a long surgical scar.
Both of them sag like worn out chairs,
something in them, habit maybe,
holding them up against all probability.
When they count their losses
they must count themselves
lucky to be here, shivering by the pool.

But when they take to the water,
mostly water themselves, they ripple
through it, stroking easily, slowly,
one end to the other, then back again,
and the water takes them as its own,
lifting them, cradling them in
its cool, familiar weightlessness.

The Philosophy of the Motel Pool

After the travelers have all gone to bed,
the motel pool settles into its blues.
The filter motor goes quiet, and the water
stops moving. Everyone who has been there
was just passing through. Empties and ashtrays,
candy wrappers, someone's lost flip-flops
or tank top or towel or fashion magazine—

in the soft glow from the underwater lights these
things lie around the deck like fragments of dreams,
bits of evidence at a crime scene,
but the pool itself is unperturbed.
The woman who swam laps early
and the man who stopped to watch her
are both gone. The family of four from Omaha,

the honeymoon couple, silly with champagne,
and the boy who played frogman all afternoon
will not be back again. No matter who dives in,
no matter how they splash or agitate,
every night the pool resolves
to be flat, placid. It is not depressed.
It's only doing what water does at a time like this.

One Night on Bainbridge Island

After the reception, I fell in with the others
leaving by the path across the Bloedel estate.
It was already dark, but someone asked me if I'd seen
the meditation garden there, the boulders in raked sand.
I said, yes, it resembled a pond
where rocks had been dropped and the ripples caught
before they could spread across the water.

Then everyone was quiet for a while,
and I took their silence to be a reflection
of the image I had made—perfect
surface held in that passing instant
when its disturbance first begins—
and it pleased me to imagine
I could capture their thoughts like that

until someone else said the sand and boulders filled
the swimming pool where Theodore Roethke died.
The air was cool and still, and I could feel
the gravel crunching beneath my feet
and hear the others' footsteps as they walked.
No one spoke again until we reached the parking lot,
where we said good-bye and got our cars unlocked.

The Back Float

A string of bright triangular flags
hangs above the pool to tell
backstroke swimmers where the wall is,
but the woman floating beneath them now
keeps her eyes closed most of the time.
She hardly moves, kicking just a little,
barely fluttering her hand,

almost the way my mother swam
in the final depth of a coma,
the small muscles of her fingers
intermittently flickering, her lips
and eyelids flinching as if someone
had splashed her face or a fly had landed
on her cheek and she couldn't brush it away.

Suspended in the smooth, white pool
of her bed, she would gasp,
then relax, letting her breath escape,
and wait so long to take another
that I would think she had finally gone under.
It was a slow time, the whole room
floating in the clarity of one moment.

It Can Be Anything

What you see in David Hockney's pools is the water,
rarely the light reflected from it on a window or wall.
Even when light throws a net over it, the reticulated
water moves while the world around it holds still:
a boxy California house, two ridiculous spindly palms,
a diving board rigid as a plank beneath a flat blue sky,
or the painter himself tilting forward in his peach

blazer and white slacks, his expensive loafers,
stiffly contemplating the man who swims toward him
underwater. Or else there's a splash, the instant
when someone disappears and what you see is
the water leaping as if it were receiving a gift.
I have no idea what Hockney intended.
The problem is always the water

because it can be anything or nothing, like air
contained where he painted it, the abstract
in the concrete, the feeling in a hole
in the ground as water fills it, maybe
seeping unobserved into a grave
after the mourners have all gone away.
Have I ever told you why I left Los Angeles?

Ghost Trees

What Can You Say Now?
How Can You Say It?

Better to use a stick than a pen.
Better even a rock than a stick,

something inarticulate that resists
making sense. There is no sense

to make, beyond what is: our fabric
has been ripped and will not mend

though love's persistent needle
keeps trying to stitch it up again.

Farewell to John Fahey's Guitar

I hear Blind Joe Death
    has thrown it in.
Somebody thumb
    a gospel drone for him
while someone else fingers
    all the other strings
and makes them do that
    naked-wiggle thing,
that slippery bend,
    that nasty little slide.
Sounds like Blind Joe
    Death has gone and died.

In the Afterlife

Let your name be Smoke.
It will be smoke anyway
soon enough and after that

let your name be Ash.
Let wind spread your name.
Let wind make you famous

among the innumerable
particles of dust. Then
let rain come. Let rain turn

your name to mud. Let Mud
be your name like your mother
said it would be if you didn't

behave. If you didn't do what
she said. Let her say this
isn't exactly what she meant.

The Tourists

Because it is a country most of us visit
only rarely, we will never be fluent

in the language of grief. We speak haltingly
and often have to excuse ourselves, saying Sorry,

sorry. What else can we do?
Whenever we go there, although we know

we've packed more than we need,
we refuse to let anyone carry our luggage.

In the streets, we clutch new souvenirs
like wounds, as if letting go of them

even briefly would ruin us.
But no one else is going

to want what we've bought.
No one is going to pick our pockets.

Wherever we walk, even crossing the piazza,
we find ourselves alone, the architecture foreign,

the buildings all painted the same conservative shades
as the shirts of undertakers. We are always getting lost.

And when we come back home again, none
of our friends will ask to see our photographs.

Instead, they'll want to try out the few clumsy words
they can remember from their own trips across that border.

Missing Richard

is like reaching for a book,
knowing the color of the dust jacket
and how it had gotten a little worn at the corners
and how the title ran sideways down the spine
saying its name, saying *Richard* in this case.

But it's not on the shelf where it was
supposed to be, and it isn't on any other shelf or among
the books stacked on chairs or on the table or on the floor.
If only you could pick it up and open it now,
you swear you would read every word again, slowly.

Little Finger

> Like most women her age, she traditionally cuts off
> a finger each time a relative or close friend dies.
> —Phil Borges, from the caption to his photograph
> of Enalia, 50, Jiwika, Irian Jaya, in *Enduring Spirit*

I was the first to go,
the runt of the left hand
litter, smallest of the lot,
but not necessarily the least
important or weakest.

I was her booger hooker,
her eye-corner cleaner,
the wax extractor
for her left ear.
I picked out secrets

that I would never tell.
You might have known me
anywhere by my nail,
my hook, my crooked
knuckle, before I fell.

Who can say what the living
will endure? I remember how,
wringing a chicken's neck, I felt it give.
I was a pioneer. I was the first to go.
I know what it means to be lonely.

My Mother Is in the Trunk

of someone's '37 Plymouth, Oklahoma plates,
trunk lid off its hinges. She's wrapped in a quilt,
riding with the cots, the tent, the picnic basket,
her face as radiant as a hubcap.

I think she must think she's getting away
with something. She hasn't yet been anywhere
near the place where I'll wind up scattering her ashes.
In fact, it will be ten more years before I matter at all,

before she even thinks of me. From here I can't tell
who is behind the wheel, who is aiming the lens,
who wants to get on with it and who it is
that wants this one moment to hold still.

Meeting the Night Visitors

Forget about them. That's the best
thing to do. If you plan on meeting them,
they probably won't come. You can burn
all the candles you want, but they still won't
sit at your table. Perhaps some other time,
the house quiet, your reading light
a pool where your book, your boat drifts,
one of them might float up almost as close
as your shoulder, but if you turn around
it's all over. No one's there.

They startle you when they do reveal themselves,
these figures lingering on the periphery of vision,
planting suggestions that you almost think you hear:
Be not afraid and *Glad tidings*, and all that.
But they never turn up when you want them,
won't get you out of trouble when you call.
Instead, they'll slip around behind you in the dark,
thinner than mist, making you shiver,
maybe warning you not to look at all,
maybe threatening to turn you to salt.

Waking from the Dream of   Obligation & Progress

It was slow-going, pedaling his unicycle
up that steep path toward the schoolyard,
and he was already running late.
Overhead, the sun had swollen
into a white blister, and now the bunches
of bright flowers he clutched in both hands
were beginning to wilt. These he was to deliver
to someone whose name he could not remember
though he thought he might yet recall it,
so he pressed on, his unicycle weaving
its tedious way up the rocky hill
one jerky foot at a time. The children
behind the chain link fence grinned
and giggled, shouting at him in some
dialect he couldn't quite decipher,
flapping their arms to mimic the way
he waved his flowers around for balance.
But his own children would not be there.
He dimly remembered that they had grown
up and moved away from home,
that he, himself, had never owned a unicycle,
never even tried to ride one, and anyway
he could think of no one who expected him
to deliver those worn-out flowers.

She Falls for It Over & Over

Memory says, Guess again:
Which hand? Then switches
whatever it's holding.

It scrambles her recipes,
teaspoon & tablespoon,
pinch & cup,

steals salt from the shaker,
leaves sugar in its place,
an April fool waiting for her to taste

the clam chowder she would have made
if memory hadn't done something
with the clams.

When she thinks of the joke about
how we could have made an omelet
if only we had eggs,

it slips away, then pops
back up for her to tell again,
and she falls for it over & over:

We could have made clam chowder
if we only had scrambled clams.
If only she had a cup

of something that would stay
in its place, like flour,
like salt she could pinch & throw

over her shoulder for luck—but no.

Days from now the clams will turn up
stinking in a cupboard & the milk will

ripen overnight in the microwave
while memory says, Guess again,
guess again: Which hand?

In the Last Place

Whatever fits together comes apart.
At least, that's how he always looks
at a problem—a frozen bolt, a stuck lock,
a stopped lawnmower—as if some quirk,
some wrinkle of his brain makes him see
any object in its exploded view: the leaky
bucket laid out as rivets, wire, and tin;
the clock as cogs and springs, face and hands.
Politics? money. Love? electricity.
And she is clipped coupons, fruit in jars.

But something new has gotten into her,
something he can't explain. A dropped
stitch. A boiled egg in a cereal box,
spoiling in a closet. Her lost pocketbook
turning up in the oven. The bathroom
cabinet spilling used facial tissues.
She puts her lipstick on to wash the dishes.
He puzzles over the way she's changed,
the way she's stayed the same as she was,

but these are still the days of saved pennies,
salvaged parts. Whatever can be dismantled
can be fixed. The answer is sure to be
so obvious he didn't think of it.
Lost things surface in the last place you look.
In the clock on the kitchen wall. In the electric
hours, time running on love as it does
in the face of the microwave, green
light-emitting diodes glowing
bright as hope above the stove.

Heart's Desire

Maybe all it really wants is to be
appreciated. Maybe it's just tired
of keeping the beat—*ba-boom, ba-boom*.
If you had to do that, wouldn't you slip-
in a paradiddle? A couple of rim shots?

Or maybe it's jealous, afraid
you'll give it away. Possessive, clinging,
squeezing so hard you can't breathe,
it's murmuring, *Baby, Baby, wherever I go,
you know I'm taking you with me.*

What You Can Say to Me When I'm Dead

I won't want to talk about the war,
so don't start. I won't say anything at all
about politics. I've already had it

up to here with gossip.
And God is no good, either,
as a conversational topic. I'll be finished,

too, with gnawing on the dry bones
of art, of accomplishment.
You can put them into your own

soup if you feel like it. I'll be lying
down for a while. Just fill me in
on what you've been up to.

The Winter Solstice

Trees in fog, like stick
figures scribbled on tissue
as if someone were

trying to design
them from scratch—ghost trees, empty
coat hangers of trees—

without knowing how.
Therefore nothing is resolved.
Soon it will be dark.

After the Fire

> I wake up in my dream. I'm wide awake
> asleep on Outer Drive.
> —Robert Huff

I don't want to think of him waking up
in a flaming chair, in a fiery shawl, howling.
God, that man could roar! I can hear him still
over whiskey, through his smoke,
bellowing across my kitchen table
You think that's poetry? then quoting
Auden, how the Old Masters were never wrong,
shoving me into the way the poem worked,
stuffing his mouth with the salmon I had cooked,
the beans I'd picked and snapped that afternoon.

He could move with the sympathetic rhythms
of birds, their migratory flights, their seasonal habits,
winging it from wreck to wreck,
one poem to another, one illusion to the next,
playing his tricks of the mouth on the ear,
playing paradox: waking in a dream, or wide awake
sleeping-off something in his blood.
The last time I saw him, I left him there for good,

and when I heard of the dropped cigarette,
the burning chair, his dying in the fire,
I felt like a traitor. I took the news away
to Inis O'irr, where miles of dry stone walls
divide the island into tiny farm plots, tracing
the contours of rock and rift
and local economy. There I walked
the boreens all day and never saw anyone

farming. Still, everywhere I went
those walls, their curious order,
even the weeds between them
said someone had been there
working, making sense.

Dolmen

What endures
does so because it can:

these massive stones left standing
in a field where someone stood them
centuries ago, another slab of stone lying
across them, sloping like a shed roof.

But what endures is more than stone.

It slips away
when crowds of tourists come
taking turns taking pictures
of themselves beside the tomb.

It comes back when they're gone.

Someone alone in the field at dawn
or on a foggy winter evening
might feel it, stiller than hedgerows,
thinner than smoke.

Whatever it is
belongs to that place.
It seems to prefer the rain.

Drâa Valley Cemetery

Pounded flat by habit
a narrow path leaves a pile
of houses pulled from the ground
brick on brick and crumbling back
since the day they were made.

Beyond the last wall, sharp stones
mark the ends of graves as if to say
dry loss makes plain sorrow harder.
Whatever grows there grows
thorns, comes bent from the seed,

endures because it must.
Because there is no real comfort
in a coffin. Because there is
no coffin at all, just someone
wound in a shroud,

carried out from the town.
Parched air hovers around the graves,
and hoopoes probe the dirt between
stones, stop and hold—then flash
black wing stripes, bright topknots

into the green relief of the palmerie
across the road. Its irrigated shade.
New wheat coming up beneath the trees.
Whatever you thought you were
made of was never meant to last.

White Scar

Vapor Trail

At dusk, an airliner carves a white scar
across the sky and I try to imagine going
somewhere myself but end up right
here, thinking anyone with a window seat

could be looking out over my town, with its
houses, streetlights, the headlights of moving
cars, the sidewalk where I'm standing still,
tiny down here, really insignificant, after all.

Come Again?

No matter where I go I think of somewhere
else, some place I've traveled in the past.
In Morocco, breathing dry Saharan air,
I saw Sonora with its cactus and its dust.

If every single place must have its double
and every double doubles-up the same,
then here, with my elbows on this table,
I could still be anywhere but where I am.

As I Walked Out One Morning

In the vacant lot where something had been
demolished and hauled away to make

room for something else that was
never built, a white plastic shopping bag

floated on an updraft, swirling past
a leggy pink bougainvillea and falling

indecisively, flexing like a jellyfish.
Glass fragments sparkled where it landed

among the bits of brick, broken concrete,
thrown-away paper, crushed cardboard boxes,

and nearly hidden in the weeds behind
the only tree, a man lay with his face in the dirt,

shoulder seam of his jacket ripped, arms
outstretched, hands open as if he had just dived in

and now was doing the deadman's float.
No one on the sidewalk seemed to notice him.

Foreign

In his own mouth the sound
of someone else's language was

as surprising as being kissed
by a total stranger and feeling

her tongue suddenly begin
to squeeze between his teeth.

Even the simplest encounter left him
wondering what he'd said, exactly,

just before that moment
parted its lips.

The Kon Tum Motorbike Taxi Driver

says before the city fell he lived
in Saigon. He says he is sorry
his English is not better. He says
he has more practice now with French.
He says he used to be a professor of
philosophy. He says that was before . . .
and he waves his hand as if he were
brushing away a bothersome fly.
He says he went to America once.
He says that was also before . . .
and the same fly requires
brushing away. He says he is sure
you know what he is saying.

Everything But the Squeal

Loops of stripped intestine
roped over themselves beside
hearts, livers, kidneys, ribs,
legs with the trotters still on,
and a pile of something like
chops, but what got to me
there inside the Kon Tum
public market was a face peeled
right off its skull and spread out
flat, ear to pointy ear, a pink
mask but sort of friendly,
mouth open wide beneath
the snout, the eyeholes surprised.

Once I might have thought it
would be funny to try it on, maybe
snort a little, stick out my tongue,
but now I couldn't even take
a surreptitious photograph,
the meaty air a gag, a wet rag
tied around my mouth, the heat
hog-thick, flies lighting
wherever no one was fanning them
away. And no one was fanning them
away. Not there. Not outside, either,
where the shade was melting
around the last few hostages,
tight in their wire baskets.

Sukulen, the Predictor

> Two months before I arrived, she had told several
> people in her village that I was coming, and had
> described in detail my appearance and the equipment
> I was using.
> —Phil Borges, from the caption to his photograph of
> Sukulen, 37, Mt. Nyiru, Kenya, in *Enduring Spirit*

When she closes her eyes she sees
far across the curve of the plain

between the scrubby trees
and the dust that bathes them.

She does not know how to pronounce your name,
but she has heard what the crows have said

about you. The crows did not speak
your language, although they tried

to approximate it anyway, saying money.
Saying comfort. Saying anything but hunger.

Saying your world is tall and shiny
even at night. That it hums like a hundred

bees in a jar. That it unravels
the yarn of all promises.

That even now it does not know how to fall.
That even now it is falling,

one feather at a time out of dry clouds.
But the crows would only say so much.

She does not know if it will all come down at once.
She does not know what will happen if it does.

At least you are out of it for now, your wheels
rolling toward her across the scoured ground.

The Legless Shoeshine Man

has a scrap of corrugated
cardboard on the sidewalk
where he sits so his stumps
almost appear to be knees
behind his box of paste polish
and dye. As he rubs and buffs,
his brush remembers how
feet feel inside their shoes.

Cut-Away View of a Trailer
South of Mérida

First, behold the man: bald spot probable
beneath his baseball cap, sweat darkening
his shirt, stomach swelling over his belt,
face flaming with sunburn, with fury,

and his wife trying to calm him down,
pull him back from the road as a bus
slows to pass. But he has to look. His pickup,
half on the pavement, and his trailer,

still loaded but open, one whole side peeled
back like the lid of an anchovy can, exposing
the inside of their closet, their bathroom,
their made bed, their cabinets packed

with dishes, pots & pans, a marvel
of efficiency, neat as a boat, sailing
nowhere. And out of that same destination
this audience of straw hats, machetes,

wide brown faces. Some of them
examining the stock truck on the opposite
shoulder, the instrument of his misery,
its own damage mostly the alarmed

bellowing, stamping of the cattle,
the cracked bed stakes stout enough
to hold the rest of the way to slaughter.
And the bus creeping past,

its curious windows peering down
on him as he swears to God somebody is
going to pay, though no one around here
will ever have that kind of money.

Now You See It, Now You Don't

A Chinese woman recites a poem in Chinese
about the moon—how it is the same moon
here as the one she would have seen
at night in the sky above China, how seeing it
now connects her to the family she left behind.

The sound of her voice rises and falls
like the flight of a swallow across a quiet pond,
climbing, diving, almost dipping into the water,
then swooping up suddenly again along the shore.

But when she translates
the poem, tells you what it means,
there is no swallow flying through it.
All you can see is this one
true thing about the moon.

The Town at the Bottom of the Reservoir

They had a post office and a general store
with gas pumps out front, and you could buy
cold Cokes there, or beer or bait or a Sunday newspaper,
mantles for your Coleman lantern, canned beans,
wieners, whatever you'd need if you were going on upstream.
In summer, sunglasses from the carousel rack, block ice.
In the winter, gloves, rock salt, antifreeze.
Down the street they had a chainsaw shop
where you could get bar oil or caulks
or have somebody fix your saw if it wouldn't start.
They had a tavern, a cafe that served a Logger's
Special with bottomless coffee, and they had a church.

But the power company's engineers said
this valley was the ideal place to build a dam.
If you lived here you could have let them
buy your house, or you might have tried to hold out,
but it was all the same. No matter how you fought
or who you called, pretty soon the digging began
and then there was no stopping it. Still sometimes
in a dry year the water drops far enough to let you see
how things have been getting along since then.
Aside from the mud it really doesn't look all that bad.

What a World

Faint moon coming up over the hills,
late sun bleeding like red Madras cloth
into pale laundry piled along the opposite horizon,
the water a sheet of hammered copper, the breeze

dying—an hour from now it will be perfectly still.
All of the afternoon's sailboats will have slipped
past on their way back to the docks,
and atop the derelict pilings the osprey they disturbed

will be settled in her nest again,
the last of her warning cries lost,
having pierced the thick fabric of dusk,
having gotten away.

This is not what we usually mean
when we look at one another and say *What a world!*
But suppose it were, and everyone, all of us,
spent every moment noticing.

Dans le Jardin El Harti, Marrakech

All winter the dry fountains,
and now the sound of water
spilling into them. It fills
the shade, fools it toward coolness,
blends with the intentional dissonance
of flamenco from the pavilion. Impromptu
guitar and palmas and someone wringing
sorrow out of the air. Girls practicing
a posture they aren't supposed to know,
as they aren't supposed to notice
the boys hanging out around the plaza.
Their Spanish haircuts. Their American-
style jeans. Two maintenance men
wearing floppy straw hats adjust the aim
of a sprinkler on the grass and flake out
a length of industrial yellow hose.
Once my son's saxophone teacher said
Look, if he thinks you're listening
he won't really practice, he'll just be
showing off. I watch the water,
what it keeps making of itself
where it falls. The glittering curtain of it
stippling the lawn, the dark map
where it splatters onto the walk.
The maintenance men never stop.
They adjust another faucet and move on,
and the couple seated on the nearest green
bench act as if they don't care who sees them,
the way they discreetly touch, the way
they give their attention to each other,
she wearing a hijab and he in a white
djellaba so brilliant it splinters the light.
But they do not move, even when

the voice of the muezzin floats
between the olive trees, calling them.
There is no god but God. There is no law
but Allah. No blessing more
transformative than water. For months
these fountains have been as wasted
as vacant hotels. Cracked concrete
collecting trash. But now this splashing.
This racket of blackbirds, of bulbuls
in the foliage overhead. It's hard to tell
who is showing off, who is
supposed to be the audience.
When I first arrived in this city I thought
I was really getting somewhere.

The Terrible Confusion of Light

Good News

     tends to get lost
amid falling stocks, bricks,
     washed-up prospects,

the general television
     din, the whole racket
of catastrophe. But it's still

     here in a backyard
garden, in beans and squash
     and someone itching

to get them into the kitchen.
     Someone lingering
later over the dishes,

     thinking of the meal as
a marriage. Wanting the taste of it
     to last and last and last.

The Nature Poem

hears you approaching
on your two clumsy feet and slips
deeper into the cover of its thicket

or crawls farther under its rock.
It holds still there until you've given up,
then it comes back out to track you.

Wherever you are, stop.
Listen hard. Right now,
it might even have you surrounded.

Nice Hat

Under bright moonlight the antlers
of a blacktail buck turn and rise
from the patch of wild raspberries
growing on the slope behind my house

and turn and fall back into it
like the forked masts of a dream
ship sinking, surfacing, sinking
repeatedly on a calm sea.

Wrapped in their blood-rich velvet,
still hardening, they are already magnificent,
those antlers, and for a moment I wish
I could have them growing from my own head.

Then I'd never again be at a loss
for a way to start a conversation,
yet in department meetings or at cocktail parties
everyone would give me plenty of room.

I could make my own space in crowded bars,
be seated right away in busy restaurants,
speed through supermarket quick-check lines.
No one would want to keep me waiting behind them.

And if I ever had to argue a difficult position,
I could swing my antlers around for emphasis,
heft them for rhetorical leverage.
I could even make several points at once.

Now the buck in the berry thicket lifts his head, dips it again, and I think of the way I've been trying to speak to you. Suppose I simply bowed respectfully. Surely that would get your attention.

Out of Season

Snow on the way but
still, this hummingbird, busy
first with the empty

nectar feeder, then
with the rosemary beside
the driveway. It too

is late, flowering
after a frost. Persistent
and optimistic.

Greeting the Hummingbirds

> Flight biomechanics researchers found, by capturing
> the breath of a hummingbird flying in a wind tunnel,
> that male hummingbirds expend negligibly more
> energy on flight when their tail feathers are extended
> to five times normal length.
> —"Findings," *Harper's Magazine*, June 2009

As it turns out they sometimes winter here
so the one I saw mid-December, snow falling,
the one I said would be a frozen goner soon
might have been the same bird I saw at the empty feeder

in March, the one that prompted me to say it seemed
awfully early in the season. But here he was, bright
throat flashing & wings a green smear in the air,
spark-quick tongue a little sputter

at the tip of his matchstick beak. Punch line
to the joke of my ignorance. I know nothing
about the biomechanics of flight. Catching the breath
of hummingbirds in wind tunnels. Measuring

the energy they expend. Never mind
the length of their tail feathers. Seeing them
again I say, Welcome back from wherever
you were in all your unlikely shining.

Origami

A thousand folded cranes
holding a single wish.
So many long-necked birds
carrying prayers as
fragile as the paper
they're made of,
                    but last night
they flew over my house
trailing their skinny legs,
and they were rattling some
dry message back and forth
between them, a prickly
seed ball, a bomb they could
neither drop nor swallow.

Loggerheads

The sandspit aimed its finger
to accuse the cool blue moving
sea of indifference because

someone had hung the thick skulls
of turtles nearby in a bleached bare tree,
its branches holding their bony weight

the way a crooked spine would
cable to a brain in the privacy
of its own container,

and still the water stayed cool, stayed
blue, though the only remaining shade was
hiding inside those wide eye sockets,

the white caves where it collected itself,
holding still, at rest
amid the terrible confusion of light.

The Boys

> Hiroshima is famous all over Japan for its association with the neighbouring islet of Itaku-Shima, Island of Light . . .
> —*Encyclopædia Britannica*, 1959

We dropped our little boy off
and an island of light fell on the city.
It flashed our enemies into light as well
or turned them to ash or cooked and skinned them alive,
left them trailing the ribbons of their faces
as they ran, panicked through their ruined streets.

We'd given him our blessing and we'd let him fly
or fall on his own. He was a huge success.
So we sent his fat brother down right away
to spread the same light in another place.
Oh, those two boys had a promise so bright it blinded us.

The Hiroshima Day Sidewalk Silhouettes

This could be anyone
spread out here flat as a map,
a Rorschach blot, a thought gelling into
a continent.
          White chalk: I think
of how it powders your fingers, sucks
the moisture out of your skin, the dry
whisper it makes, thin squeal
of nails, quick shiver telegraphed
tooth to spine.
            This could be anyone
flattened here, blasted down to shadow.
So why am I drawn to look again
each time I turn away?
              No matter
what I know, somebody knows it better.
Neutrons, electrons. The hot rods
in the containment shell. Geologic
faults. Cracked concrete, this chalk
drawing on it, harmless as hopscotch now
in the part of the world I walk around in.

These Others

the men in the river
the men who had been standing
    on the bank before they dove
        into the blue dream of history
all tried to save themselves
all scattered when the others attacked them
    when the others covered them
    in a furious swarm of arrows

but no matter where they ran
    these men on the bank of the river
they ran toward more arrows
and no matter how they swam
    these men in the river
        they had to come up for air

    and when they opened their mouths
    they opened their mouths to arrows

when the others were finished
    they lowered their bows
when they finished
    they had arrows to spare
each with its point hidden in the quiver
    its fletched end
        ready as a winged idea

when they finished
    they praised what they had done
        they said it had to be
and then they sat down to eat

or they drank till they were drunk
or they found someone to fuck
or they prayed they gave thanks
    to one god or another
        these others with their arrows

Resolution

Afterward, the crows
perching in the bare orchard
rattled black vowels,

broken consonants
from their feathered bags as if
they'd seen all there was

to see, had said so
over and over: the old
complaints, grown heavy,

overripe, had dropped.
New recruits stooped, picked them up.
Eager to begin,

optimistic as
saints, they said surely the worst
was over. But no,

it would start again
the same way for them. Let them
have it. Let them be

among the lucky;
let their dead give up their tongues.
Let the last owl in

the dry, brown woods keep
calling out the same hollow
vowels all night long.

Acknowledgments & Notes

Many thanks to the editors of the publications where these poems previously appeared, often in somewhat different versions:

5 AM: "Meeting the Night Visitors."

Beyond Forgetting: Poetry and Prose about Alzheimer's Disease, Kent State University Press: "She Falls for It Over & Over."

Caffeine Destiny: "It Can Be Anything" and "One Night on Bainbridge Island" (both reprinted in *LitSpeak Dresden*, in Germany).

Crab Creek Review: "After the Fire," "Origami" (as "Cranes"), "Man on Ice," "Nice Hat," "On the Job," and "What a World" (reprinted in *Northwest Coast*).

Crosscurrents (WCCHA): "Foreign," "Heart's Desire," and "The Old Masters" (reprinted in *LitSpeak Dresden*).

Fine Madness: "Waking from the Dream of Obligation & Progress."

Free Lunch: "Dolmen" (reprinted in *Departures: New Series*, Co. Clare, Ireland), "Little Finger," and "Sukulen, the Predictor."

Hubbub: "My Mother Is in the Trunk," "Resolution," "The Back Float" and "Waterbabies" (both reprinted in *LitSpeak Dresden*), and "Why Did the Hawk Cross the Road?"

Jeopardy: "The First Day" (reprinted in *LitSpeak Dresden*), "The Hiroshima Day Sidewalk Silhouettes" and "Loggerheads" (as "The Turtles of Isla Mujeres").

Kudzu: A Digital Quarterly: "The Boys," "The Philosophy of the Motel Pool" (reprinted in *Pontoon* and *LitSpeak Dresden*), and "The Tourists" (reprinted in *Pontoon*).

Permafrost: "The Business of Crows" and "Now You See It, Now You Don't."

Pontoon: "In the Last Place" (reprinted in *Love Is Ageless: Stories About Alzheimer's Disease*, Lompico Creek Press; and *Lost and Found*, Plymouth Writers Group), and "These Believers."

The Stony Thursday Book, Limerick, Ireland: "What You Can Say to Me When I'm Dead."

Terrain.org: A Journal of the Built + Natural Environments: "Drâa Valley Cemetery," "The Kon Tum Motorbike Taxi Driver," and "Come Again?"

Wilderness: "The Nature Poem"

ZYZZYVA: "Missing Richard" and "The Jealous Gods" (reprinted in *Jump Start: A Northwest Renaissance Anthology*, Steel Toe Books).

The epigraph to "After the Fire" is from "Napping by the Sea with Sally," by Robert Huff, *The Ventriloquist: New and Selected Poems*, University Press of Virginia, 1977.

The epigraphs to "Little Finger" and "Sukulen, the Predictor" are taken from Phil Borges's collection *Enduring Spirit* and appear here with the permission of Phil Borges (Phil Borges Studio Inc., www.philborges.com) and Bridges to Understanding (www.bridgesweb.org).

Blind Joe Death is the title of guitarist John Fahey's first album on Takoma Records, released in 1959.

The poem "These Others" is a response to Ricker Winsor's painting "Escape."

"What Can You Say Now? How Can You Say It?" was first written for Karen Turner, who died far too young, but it has filled-in for lost words at other partings as well.

"Good News" is for Don and Judy Fuller.

An earlier version of "Missing Richard," for Dick Irwin, is in *Joseph Green, Greatest Hits 1975–2000*. The revised poem appears here in memory of Richard M. Kelley, who is sorely missed.

Farewell, also, to Ron Offen, whose post-it notes and correspondence helped to nudge many of these poems into shape, whether he ultimately published them or not. Without him, there really is no more *Free Lunch*.

Thanks, again and again, to PEN Northwest, John Daniel, and the Boyden family for the Margery Davis Boyden Wilderness Writing Residency at Dutch Henry Homestead, the birthplace of "The Nature Poem" and "Nice Hat."

Finally, a deep bow of gratitude to Lana Hechtman Ayers for her patience and persistence in bringing this book forward.

About the Author

Joseph Green has held writing residencies in Oregon and Spain, traveled to Vietnam three times, and taken extended visits to Mexico, Ireland, and Morocco. His poems have been appearing in magazines and journals since 1975, and many are collected in *His Inadequate Vocabulary* (The Signpost Press), *Deluxe Motel* (The Signpost Press), *Joseph Green, Greatest Hits 1975—2000* (Pudding House), *The End of Forgiveness* (Floating Bridge Press), and *That Thread Still Connecting Us* (MoonPath Press).

What Water Does at a Time Like This includes uncollected work from the last twenty-five years along with new poems, all revisited, often reworked, and considered in regard to the company they keep within these pages.

In addition to writing, Joseph Green prints limited-edition poetry broadsides with hand-set metal type at The Peasandcues Press, in Longview, Washington; and in Portland, Oregon, he serves on the board of directors for the C.C. Stern Type Foundry.